CW01081247

AIR FRYER
COOKBOOK FOR BEGINNERS

1001 Easy Air Fryer Recipes on a Budget
for Beginners, including popular family
meals

-By-

Jenny T Scott

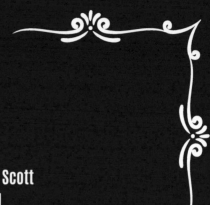

© Copyright 2022 –Jenny T Scott
Every right is reserved.

The contents of this book may not be duplicated, copied, or transferred without the author's or publishers express written consent. The publisher or author of this book will not be held responsible or liable for any harm, compensation, or financial loss that comes directly or indirectly from the information in this book.

Important Legal Information

Copyright protects this book. It is solely meant for personal use. You can't change, copy, sell, use, quote, or paraphrase any part of this work without the author's or publisher's permission.

Disclaimer Statement

Please keep in mind that the material in this booklet is solely for educational and entertaining purposes. Every attempt has been made to offer information that is accurate, up-to-date, dependable, and thorough. There is no express or implied guarantee of any sort. The reader knows that the author doesn't give professional advice in areas like law, finance, medicine, or other fields.

This book's material was compiled from a number of sources. Before trying any of the practises mentioned in this book, please get the advice of a qualified expert. By reading this document, the reader agrees that the author is not responsible for any direct or indirect damages that come from using the information in it, including but not limited to mistakes, omissions, or inaccurate information.

Table of contents

BREAKFAST RECIPES...7

SCRAMBLED OREGANO AND COCONUT...7
EGGS, SPINACH, AND CHEESE 7
TOAST WITH STRAWBERRIES 8
OMELETTE WITH CHIVES 8
BAKED EGGS 9
CINNAMON-SWEET POTATO TOAST...9
A HOLE-IN-ONE 10
MUFFINS WITH SAUSAGE AND EGGS 10
GRILLED SAUSAGES ON THE BBQ 11
SIMPLE SALT AND PEPPER STEAK, MEDIUM RARE..11
TOFU TAJ...12
CINNAMON BUNS 12
PIZZA WITH EGGS 13
BREAD WITH WHITE WHEAT AND WALNUTS 13
TOAST CUPS WITH HAM AND EGGS 14
BACON CRISPS...15
GRAVY FROM THE COUNTRY 15
BREAD FRY 16

APPETIZERS AND SNACKS 17

CHIPS MADE FROM CARROTS 17
CRISPY RAVIOLI BITES 17
ROUNDS OF CHEDDAR 18
ONION RINGS WRAPPED IN BACON..18
OLIVES FRIED...19
CHIPS MADE WITH FRIED KALE 20
FRIES TOPPED WITH AVOCADO 20
ROLL-UPS OF CRISPY SALAMI...21
FRENCH FRIES WITH BUFFALO SAUCE 21
ROASTED PEANUTS..22
GARLIC-CREAM WONTONS WITH CHEESE 22
CROUTONS 23
SPINACH DIPPING SAUCE..23
GRILLED BELL PEPPERS 24
CHIPS MADE WITH KALE...24

BEEF -PORK & LAMB RECIPES..25

PROVENÇAL GRILLED RIB-EYE 25
DOGS ON A STICK 25
BEEF ROAST 26
LAMB CHOPS WITH ROSEMARY 26
THESE CHEESEBURGERS ARE DELICIOUS 27
MEATBALLS FROM ITALY 27
LAMB ROAST 28
BURGERS WITH BACON AND BLUE CHEESE 28
A BURGER WITH BACON AND BLUE CHEESE 29
MEATLOAF 29
GRILLED FIGS WITH PROSCIUTTO 30
CHOPS OF LAMB 30

POULTRY RECIPES 31

WINGS OF CHICKEN 31
TURKEY BREAST WITH HERB SEASONING 32
CHICKEN BREASTS WITH SWEET NUTTY SAUCE 32
NACHOS WITH BAKED CHICKEN 33
THE FINEST GRILLED CHICKEN BREAST 33
CHICKEN THIGHS WITH CINNAMON 34
PARTRIDGE, ROSEMARY 34
CRISPY & EASY CHICKEN WINGS 35
CHICKEN BREASTS (BASIC) 35
SANDWICHES WITH BUFFALO CHICKEN 36
CHICKEN WITH CREAMY ONION SAUCE 36
QUICK CHICKEN FILLING 37
CHICKEN BREAST WITH LEMON PEPPER 37
CHICKEN AND BACON WRAPPED 38
TERIYAKI CHICKEN LEGS 38
CHICKEN WINGS WITH BUFFALO SAUCE 39
TURKEY NUGGETS WITH THYME 39

FISH AND SEAFOOD RECIPES 40

SCALLOPS WITH A SWEET-AND-SPICY CURE 40
SEA BASS WITH LEMON AND THYME 41
SALMON WITH MAPLE BUTTER 41
QUICK AND EASY LIME-GARLIC SHRIMP 42
CAPERS AND TOMATOES WITH SWORDFISH 42
SCALLOPS WITH GARLIC AND LEMON 43
FLOUNDER CUTLETS IN RESTAURANT STYLE 43
STICKS OF FISH 44

QUICK AND SIMPLE SHRIMP 44

CAJUN LOBSTER TAILS 45

HADDOCK WITH HERBS 45

FILLETS OF FRIED CATFISH 46

BAKED COD IN ITALIAN SAUCE 46

INCREDIBLE CRISPY FRIED SALMON SKIN 47

SIMPLE LOBSTER TAIL WITH BUTTER 47

SALMON FILLETS WITH LEMON ROASTING 48

BURGERS WITH SHRIMP 48

NUGGETS OF COD 49

FILLETS OF TILAPIA 50

CAJUN SCALLOPS WRAPPED IN BACON 50

VEGETARIANS RECIPES 51

WINGS WITH ALMOND FLOUR BATTER 51

1 CUP BELL PEPPERS 51

GOURMET WASABI POPCORN 52

ROASTED SPAGHETTI SQUASH 52

GREEN BEANS WITH LEMON 53

WITH OLIVES, BROCCOLI 53

CAULIFLOWER WITH BROCCOLI 54

BROCCOLI SALAD 54

AVOCADO WRAPS 55

AIR FRYER SKEWERED CORN 55

GREEN BEANS FROM THE GARDEN 56

APPLE-LICIOUS APPLE CHIPS 56

VEGETABLE SIDE DISHES RECIPES 57

CHILLI OIL BRUSSELS SPROUTS 57

ROASTED BRUSSELS SPROUTS 57

ASPARAGUS 58

FRIES WITH PARMESAN AND GARLIC 58

CARROTS WITH A SAVOURY ROAST 59

ROASTED SWEET POTATOES MADE EASY 59

BUTTERNUT SQUASH FRIES ON A BUDGET 60

FRIES MADE WITH SWEET POTATOES 60

ROASTED BROCCOLI 61

MEXICAN-STYLE FRITTATA 61

DESSERTS AND SWEETS RECIPES 62

MUFFINS WITH NUTS AND FUDGE 62

COCONUT FLAKES, TOASTED 62

PASTRIES WITH MARSHMALLOWS 63

MERENGUE'S 63

APPLE BAKE 64

CHOCOLATE SOUFFLÉS 64

MARMALADE ORANGE 65

BROWNIES WITH CHOCOLATE CHIPS 65

CINNAMON-ROASTED PUMPKIN SEEDS 66

STRAWBERRIES ON CUPCAKES 66

RECIPE FOR MUG BROWNIES 67

CAKE WITH LEMON RICOTTA 67

BANANA PASTRY WITH A HEART 68

BREAD WITH MONKEYS 68

LIME MUFFINS WITH NO FLOUR 69

MIDNIGHT NUTELLA BANANA SANDWICH 69

CHOCOLATE BOMBS 70

FRUIT ROTATIONS 70

OREOS FRIED 71

TWINKIES FRIED 71

LEMON BERRIES IN A STEW 72

DELECTABLE VANILLA CUSTARD 72

BREAKFAST RECIPES

SCRAMBLED OREGANO AND COCONUT

4 servings

Time to cook: 20 minutes.

Ingredients:

- 8 whisked eggs
- 2 tsp oregano, chopped
- To taste, season with salt and black pepper.
- 2 tsp. grated parmesan
- 1/4-cup heavy cream

Directions:

1. In a mixing bowl, combine the eggs and the remaining ingredients. Pour this into an air fryer-compatible pan, place it in the prepared fryer, and cook it at 350°F for 20 minutes, stirring often. Serve the scramble in individual dishes for breakfast.

EGGS, SPINACH, AND CHEESE

2 servings

Time to cook: 40 minutes.

Ingredients:

- Three entire eggs.
- 3 ounces of cottage cheese.
- 3 to 4 ounces chopped spinach
- 1/4 cups of grated parmesan cheese
- 1/4 cup of milk

Directions:

1. Preheat the fryer to 375 degrees Fahrenheit.
2. In a large mixing bowl, combine the eggs, cottage cheese, parmesan, and milk.
3. Mix in the spinach thoroughly.
4. Arrange in a small, oiled frying pan.
5. Top with the cheese.
6. Bake at 350°F for 25-30 minutes.
7. Set aside for 5 minutes before serving.

TOAST WITH STRAWBERRIES

4 servings

Time to cook: 8 minutes.

Ingredients:

- 4 pieces of 1/2-inch thick bread.
- I flavoured cooking spray with butter.
- 1 cup sliced strawberries
- 1 teaspoon sugar

Directions:

1. Spray one side of each bread piece with butter-flavored frying spray. Place the sprayed side of the slices down.
1. Arrange the strawberries on top of the bread pieces.
2. Evenly sprinkle with sugar and arrange in an air fryer basket in a single layer.
3. Bake at 390°F for 8 minutes. The bottom should be crisp and brown, and the top should be glazed.

OMELETTE WITH CHIVES

4 servings

Time to cook: 20 minutes.

Ingredients:

- 6 whisked eggs
- 1 cup minced chives
- Spray cooking oil.
- 1 cup mozzarella shredded
- To taste, season with salt & black pepper.

Directions:

In a mixing bowl, whisk together all of the ingredients except the cooking spray. Grease an air fryer pan with cooking spray, pour in the egg mixture, smooth it out, and place it in the machine to cook at 350 °F for 20 minutes. Serve the omelette for breakfast on individual dishes.

BAKED EGGS

4 servings

Time to cook: 6 minutes.

Ingredients:

- Four huge eggs
- 1/8 tsp. black pepper
- 1/8 teaspoons of salt

Directions:

1. Preheat the air fryer to 330 degrees F. Fill the air fryer basket with four silicone muffin liners.
2. Place one egg in each silicone muffin cup. Season with black pepper & salt to taste.
3. Bake for 6 minutes at 350°F. Remove it from the oven and set it aside for 2 minutes before serving.

CINNAMON-SWEET POTATO TOAST

6 servings

Time to cook: 8 minutes.

Ingredients:

- 1 sweet potato, cut into 3/8-inch strips
- Sprinkle with spray oil.
- Cinnamon powder

Directions:

1. Preheat the air fryer to 390 degrees Fahrenheit.
2. Lightly oil the sweet potato slices on both sides. To taste, sprinkle cinnamon on both sides.
1. Arrange potato slices in a single layer in the air fryer basket.
3. Cook for 4 minutes, then flip and cook for another 4 minutes, or until the potato slices are just fork tender.

A HOLE-IN-ONE

1 serving

Time to cook: 7 minutes.

Ingredients:

- One slice bread
- 1 tablespoon soft butter
- 1 egg
- Pepper and salt.
- 1 cup Cheddar cheese, shredded
- 2 teaspoons of ham, diced

Directions:

1. Preheat the air fryer basket as well as a 6 x 6-inch baking dish to 330°F.
2. Cut a hole in the middle of the bread slice with a 2 1/2-inch-diameter biscuit cutter.
3. Butter both sides of the bread with softened butter.
4. Place a piece of bread on a baking sheet and crack an egg into the centre. Season the eggs to taste with salt and pepper.
4. 5 minutes of cooking time.
5. Turn the bread over and top with shredded cheese and ham slices.
6. Cook for 2 minutes longer, or until the yolk is done to your preference.

MUFFINS WITH SAUSAGE AND EGGS

4 servings

Time to cook: 30 minutes.

Ingredients:

- Italian sausage, 6 oz.
- 6 eggs
- 1/8 oz. heavy cream
- 3 oz. of cheese

Directions:

1. Heat the oil in a deep fryer to 350°F.
2. Grease a muffin pan lightly.
3. Cut the sausage links in half and place them in a container.
4. 4. Combine the eggs and cream in a mixing bowl and season with salt and pepper.
5. Pour the sauce over the sausages in the tin.
6. Top with the remaining egg mixture and cheese.
7. Cook for 20 minutes, or until the eggs are cooked through. Then serve!

GRILLED SAUSAGES ON THE BBQ

Servings: 3

Time to cook: 30 minutes.

Ingredients:

- Six links of sausage
- half cup bottled barbecue sauce

Directions:

1. Preheat the air fryer to 390 degrees Fahrenheit.
2. Insert the air fryer's grill pan attachment.
3. Cook the sausage links for 30 minutes on the grill.
4. Halfway through the cooking period, flip the pan.
5. Before serving, brush with prepared BBQ sauce.

SIMPLE SALT AND PEPPER STEAK, MEDIUM RARE

Servings: 3

Time to cook: 30 minutes.

Ingredients:

- 1 1/2 lb. skirt steak
- Season with salt and pepper to taste.

Directions:

1. Preheat the air fryer to 390 degrees Fahrenheit.
2. Insert the air fryer's grill pan attachment.
3. Season both sides of the skirt steak with salt and pepper.
4. Cook each batch for 15 minutes on the grill pan.
5. Halfway through the cooking period, flip the meat over.

TOFU TAJ

4 servings

Time to cook: 40 minutes.

Ingredients:

- 1 block firm tofu, pressed and cut into 1-inch thick cubes
- 2 tbsp of soy sauce
- 2 tablespoons roasted sesame seeds
- 1 tsp. rice vinegar
- 1 teaspoon corn-starch

Directions:

1. Preheat your air fryer to 400 degrees Fahrenheit.
2. In a mixing bowl, combine the tofu, soy sauce, sesame seeds, and rice vinegar and stir thoroughly to coat the tofu cubes. Then, coat the tofu with corn-starch and place it in the fryer basket.
1. Cook for 25 minutes, shaking the basket every five minutes to ensure the tofu cooks evenly.

CINNAMON BUNS

Servings: 12

Time to cook: 20 minutes.

Ingredients:

- 2 1/2 cups of shredded mozzarella cheese
- 2 oz cream cheese, softened
- 1 cup blanched almond flour, finely ground
- 1 teaspoon vanilla extract
- 1/2 cups of erythritol (confectioners')
- 1 tbsp. cinnamon powder

Directions:

1. In a large microwave-safe mixing bowl, combine the mozzarella cheese, cream cheese, and flour. Microwave the mixture for 90 seconds on high or until the cheese is melted.
2. For 2 minutes, or until a dough forms, stir in the vanilla extract and erythritol.
3. When the dough has cooled enough to handle, approximately 2 minutes, roll it out into a 12" x 4" rectangle on oiled parchment paper. Sprinkle cinnamon evenly over the dough.
4. Roll the dough lengthwise to make a log, beginning with the long side. Cut the timber into twelve equal pieces.

5. Arrange the rolls on two ungreased 6" round non-stick baking trays. Put one dish into the air fryer basket. Preheat the oven to 375°F and set the timer for 10 minutes.
6. Cinnamon buns are done when the edges are golden and the centre is generally solid. Rep with the second dish. Allow 10 minutes for the rolls to cool on their plates before serving.

PIZZA WITH EGGS

Servings: 2

Time to cook: 10 minutes.

Ingredients:

- 1 cup shredded mozzarella cheese
- 7 pepperoni slices, chopped.
- 1 large whisked egg
- 1/4 tsp. dried oregano
- 1/4 tsp. dried parsley
- 1/4 tsp. garlic powder
- 1/4 teaspoons of salt

Directions:

1. Line the bottom of a 6" round non-stick baking dish with a single layer of mozzarella. Sprinkle pepperoni on top of the cheese, and then pour the egg evenly around the baking dish.
2. Toss the remaining ingredients together and place in the air fryer basket. Set the oven temperature to 330°F and the timer for 10 minutes. When the cheese has browned and the egg has set, the dish is ready.
3. Allow the dish to cool for 5 minutes before serving.

BREAD WITH WHITE WHEAT AND WALNUTS

8 servings

Time to cook: 25 minutes.

Ingredients:

- 1 cup hot water
- 1 tablespoon Rapid Rise yeast
- 1 tablespoon light brown sugar
- 2 cups whole wheat white flour
- 1 room temperature egg, beaten with a fork.
- 2 tbsp. olive oil.
- 1/2 teaspoons of salt
- 1/2 cups of walnuts, chopped

- Sprayed frying oil.

Directions:

1. In a small mixing bowl, combine the water, yeast, and brown sugar.
2. Mix the yeast and flour together until smooth.
3. Beat in the egg, olive oil, and salt with a wooden spoon for 2 minutes.
4. Fold in the chopped walnuts. Instead of hard bread dough, you'll get a very thick batter.
5. Coat the inside of an air fryer baking pan with cooking spray and pour in the batter, smoothing the top.
6. Set aside for 15 minutes to allow the batter to rise.
1. Preheat the air fryer to 360°F.
7. Bake the bread for 25 minutes or until a toothpick inserted into the middle comes out with crumbs sticking to it. Allow the bread to rest for 10 minutes before taking it from the pan.

TOAST CUPS WITH HAM AND EGGS

Servings: 2

Time to cook: 5 minutes.

Ingredients:

- 2 eggs
- Two ham slices.
- 2 tablespoons melted butter
- Cheddar cheese as a garnish
- Season with salt to taste.
- Black pepper to taste

Directions:

1. Preheat the air fryer to 400 degrees Fahrenheit and butter both ramekins.
2. Arrange each ham slice in a greased ramekin and cover with an egg.
3. Season the air fryer basket with salt, black pepper, and cheddar cheese.
4. After 5 minutes, remove the ramekins from the basket.
5. Serve immediately.

BACON CRISPS

6 servings

Time to cook: 20 minutes.

Ingredients:

- 12 ounce of bacon

Directions:

1. Preheat the air fryer for 3 minutes at 350°F.
1. Arrange the bacon pieces in a single layer, gently overlapping them.
2. Air fry for 10 minutes, or until crispy.
3. Continue until all of the bacon is cooked.

GRAVY FROM THE COUNTRY

2 servings

Time to cook: 7 minutes.

Ingredients:

- 1/4 lb. casing-free pork sausage
- 1 tbsp. melted butter
- 2 tablespoons flour
- Two quarts whole milk
- 1/2 teaspoons of salt
- Black pepper, freshly ground.
- 1 teaspoon of thyme leaves, fresh

Directions:

1. Preheat a medium-sized pot over medium heat. Brown the sausage, breaking it up into little bits as it cooks. Stir in the butter and flour until completely combined. Cook for another 2 minutes, stirring regularly.
2. Slowly pour in the milk, whisking constantly, and heat to thicken. Season with salt and freshly ground black pepper, then reduce the heat and simmer for 5 minutes, or until the sauce has thickened to your liking. Season with salt and pepper to taste and serve the dish hot.

BREAD FRY

4 servings

Time to cook: 5 minutes.

Ingredients:

- 1 cup all-purpose flour
- 2 tbsp. baking powder.
- 1/4 teaspoons of salt
- /14 cups warmed milk
- 1 teaspoon oil
- 2 to 3 tablespoons water
- Misting oil or cooking spray

Directions:

1. In a mixing bowl, combine the flour, baking powder, and salt. Mix in the milk and oil gently. 1 tablespoon of water, stirred in If necessary, add 1 tablespoon of water at a time until a firm dough forms. Dough should not be sticky, so just use what you need.
2. Cut the dough in half and roll each half into a ball. Allow for a 10-minute rest under a towel.
3. Preheat the air fryer to 390 degrees Fahrenheit.
4. Form the dough as desired.
5. Cut the dough into 3-inch rounds. This results in thicker bread that may be eaten simply or with a sprinkling of cinnamon or honey butter. You can cook all four at the same time.
6. b. Cut into thinner 3 x 6 inch rectangles. This will result in thinner bread that may be used as a basis for meals like Indian tacos. Even though round is more common, cooking two rectangles at once in your air fryer basket is easier with rectangles.
7. Brush both sides of the dough with oil or frying spray.
8. Place 4 circles or 2 dough rectangles in the air fryer basket and cook for 3 minutes at 390°F. Spray the tops, flip them, and cook for another 2 minutes. Repeat if required to cook the remaining bread.
9. Serve immediately or allow cooling slightly before assembling your own Native American tacos.

APPETIZERS AND SNACKS

CHIPS MADE FROM CARROTS

4 servings

Time to cook: 10 minutes.

Ingredients:

- 1 pound carrots, finely sliced
- 2 tablespoons extra-virgin olive oil
- 1/4 tsp. garlic powder
- 1/4 tsp. black pepper
- 1/2 teaspoons of salt

Directions:

1. Preheat the air fryer to 390 degrees F.
2. Toss the carrot slices with the olive oil, garlic, and salt in a medium mixing bowl.
3. Salt, pepper, and powder.
4. Liberally spray the air fryer basket with olive oil mist.
5. Place the carrot slices in the basket of the air fryer. Do not overlap the carrots to ensure equal cooking; cook in batches if required.
6. Cook for 5 minutes, then shake the basket and cook for 5 minutes more.
7. Take the basket out of the oven and serve immediately. Continue with the remaining carrot slices until all of them are cooked.

CRISPY RAVIOLI BITES

5 servings

Time to cook: 7 minutes.

Ingredients:

- 1/3 cup all-purpose flour
- 1 large egg (or eggs), properly beaten
- 2/3 cup dry Italian-style seasoned bread crumbs
- 10 ounces of thawed frozen mini ravioli, meat or cheese.
- Spray with olive oil.

Directions:

1. Preheat the air fryer to 400 degrees F.
2. Place the flour in a medium mixing bowl. Fill one shallow soup plate or tiny pie plate with the beaten egg(s), and the other with the bread crumbs.

3. Coat the ravioli thoroughly in flour. Pick up 1 ravioli, brush off any excess flour, and coat both sides with the egg(s).Allow any extra egg to fall back into the remainder of the egg, then roll the ravioli in the bread crumbs, flipping several times until lightly and evenly coated on both sides. Set it aside on a chopping board while you finish the rest of the ravioli.

4. Lightly cover the ravioli on both sides with olive oil spray, and then arrange them in the basket in a single layer. Some people can lean against the basket's side. Cook for 7 minutes, flipping the basket halfway through to rearrange the pieces, until they are golden and crisp.

5. Empty the basket's contents onto a wire rack. Allow it to cool for 5 minutes before serving.

ROUNDS OF CHEDDAR

Servings: 4

Time to cook: 6 minutes.

Ingredients:

- 1 cup of Cheddar cheese, shredded

Directions:

1. Preheat the air fryer to 400 degrees F. Line the air fryer basket with parchment paper. Sprinkle the cheese in tiny circles on the baking paper. Cook for 6 minutes, or until the cheese melts and begins to crisp.

ONION RINGS WRAPPED IN BACON

2 servings

Time to cook: 30 minutes.

Ingredients:

- 1 onion, cut into 1/2-inch slices
- one tsp. curry powder
- 1 teaspoon cayenne pepper
- To taste, season with salt & black pepper.
- Eight strips of bacon
- 1/4 cup ketchup (hot)

Directions:

2. Place the onion rings in a dish of cold water and soak for 20 minutes. Drain the onion rings and wipe them dry with a kitchen towel.

3. Season onion rings with curry powder, cayenne pepper, salt, and black pepper.

4. Wrap the onion in one layer of bacon, removing any extra. Toothpicks are used to secure the rings.

5. Spray the Air Fryer basket with cooking spray and lay the breaded onion rings in it.
6. Cook for 15 minutes at 360°F in a preheated air fryer, flipping halfway through. With hot ketchup, serve. Good appetite!

OLIVES FRIED

5 servings

Time to cook: 10 minutes.

Ingredients:

- 1/3 cups of regular flour or tapioca flour
- 1 pound egg white (s)
- 1 tablespoon olive jar brine
- 2/3 cup of plain, dry bread crumbs (gluten-free if desired)
- 15 large green olives filled with pimientos
- Spray with olive oil.

Directions:

1. Preheat the air fryer to 400 degrees F.
1. Place the flour in a medium zip-top plastic bag. In a medium mixing bowl, whisk together the egg white and pickle brine until frothy. On a dinner plate, spread out the bread crumbs.
2. Place all of the olives in the bag with the flour, close it, and shake to coat. Remove a few olives, brush off any extra flour, and place them in the egg white mixture. To coat, toss lightly yet thoroughly. Pick them up one at a time and roll them in the bread crumbs, coating all sides, including the ends. Place them on a chopping board while you finish the remainder. When finished, spray the olives on both sides with olive oil spray.
3. Arrange the olives in a single layer in the basket. Air-fry the olives for 8 minutes, shaking the basket gently halfway through to move the olives around and make sure they get a light brown colour.
4. Transfer the olives to a wire rack and set them aside for at least 10 minutes before serving. Once chilled, the olives may be refrigerated in a tight container for up to 2 days. Set them aside in the basket of a hot 400°F air fryer for 2 minutes to rewarm.

CHIPS MADE WITH FRIED KALE

2 servings

Time to cook: 10 minutes.

Ingredients:

- 1 kale head, ripped into 1 1/2 inch pieces
- 1 tablespoon extra-virgin olive oil
- 1 tbsp. soy sauce

Directions:

1. Clean and dry the kale.
1. Place the kale in a mixing basin and toss with the soy sauce and oil.
2. Place it in the air fryer and cook for 3 minutes at 400 °F, stirring halfway through.

FRIES TOPPED WITH AVOCADO

4 servings

Time to cook: 20 minutes.

Ingredients:

- Half cups panko
- Half teaspoon of salt
- 1 whole avocado
- 1 quart Aquafina

Directions:

1. In a small bowl, combine the panko and salt.
1. Place the Aquafina in a separate shallow basin.
2. Coat each avocado slice in panko after dipping it in Aquafina.
3. Arrange the slices in the air fryer basket, being careful not to overlap any of them. At 390°F, air fry for 10 minutes.

ROLL-UPS OF CRISPY SALAMI

Servings: 16

Time to cook: 4 minutes.

Ingredients:

- 4 oz. cream cheese, cut into 16 equal pieces
- 16 slices of deli salami from Genoa

Directions:

1. Spread a thin layer of cream cheese around the edge of a salami slice, and then wrap it up to seal. Use a toothpick to secure it. Repeat with the remaining cream cheese and salami.
2. Place the roll-ups in the air fryer basket on an ungreased 6" round non-stick baking dish. Set the oven temperature to 350°F and the timer for 4 minutes. When done, the salami will be crispy and the cream cheese will be warm. Allow it to cool for 5 minutes before serving.

FRENCH FRIES WITH BUFFALO SAUCE

6 servings

Time to cook: 35 minutes.

Ingredients:

- 3 russet potatoes, medium
- 2 tbsp buffalo sauce
- 2 tbsp olive oil (extra virgin).
- Season with salt & pepper to taste.

Directions:

1. Preheat the air fryer to 380 degrees Fahrenheit. Peel and cut potatoes into French fries lengthwise. Put them in a basin and toss with olive oil, salt, and pepper. Air Cook for 10 minutes. Cook for 5 minutes after shaking the basket. Serve immediately with a drizzle of Buffalo sauce.

ROASTED PEANUTS

Servings: 10

Time to cook: 14 minutes.

Ingredients:

- 2 ½ cup of raw peanuts
- 1 tablespoon olive oil (extra virgin)
- Salt as needed.

Directions:

1. Preheat the air fryer to 320 degrees F.
2. Arrange the peanuts in an air fryer basket in a single layer.
3. Cook for 9 minutes in an air fryer, flipping twice.
4. Remove the peanuts from the Air Fryer basket and place them in a mixing bowl.
5. Toss in the oil and salt to thoroughly coat.
6. Return the nut mixture to the air fryer basket.
7. Air fry for about 5 minutes.
8. When finished, place the heated nuts in a glass or steel dish and serve.

GARLIC-CREAM WONTONS WITH CHEESE

4 servings

Time to cook: 8 minutes.

Ingredients:

- 6 oz. softened full-fat cream cheese.
- 1 teaspoon garlic powder
- 12 wrappers for wontons
- 1/4 cups of water

Directions:

1. Preheat the air fryer to 375 degrees F.
2. Combine cream cheese and garlic powder in a medium mixing bowl.
3. Place 1 tablespoon of cream cheese mixture in the middle of each wonton wrapper.
4. Brush the wontons' edges with water to help them seal. To make a triangle, fold the wonton. Cooking spray should be sprayed on both sides. Repeat with the rest of the wontons and cream cheese mixture.
5. Place the wontons in the air fryer basket. Cook for 8 minutes, flipping halfway through, until golden brown and crispy. Serve hot.

CROUTONS

Servings: 4

Time to cook: 5 minutes.

Ingredients:

- 4 sourdough bread slices, cut into tiny cubes.
- 2 tsp salted butter, melted
- 1 teaspoon of fresh parsley, chopped
- 2 tbsp. Parmesan cheese, grated

Directions:

1. Preheat the air fryer to 400 degrees F.
2. Combine bread cubes in a large mixing bowl.
1. Spread the butter over the bread pieces. Mix in the parsley and Parmesan. Toss the bread pieces until they are uniformly covered.
3. Arrange the bread cubes in a single layer in the air fryer basket. Cook for 5 minutes, or until well toasted. Cool completely before serving for maximum crunch.

SPINACH DIPPING SAUCE

Servings: 2

Time to cook: 15 minutes.

Ingredients:

- 8 oz. softened full-fat cream cheese
- 1/2 cups of mayonnaise
- 2 tablespoons minced garlic
- 1 cup grated Parmesan cheese
- 1 box frozen chopped spinach, thawed and drained

Directions:

1. Preheat the air fryer to 320 degrees F.
2. In a large mixing bowl, combine the cream cheese, mayonnaise, garlic, and Parmesan.
3. Stir in the spinach. Place the mixture in the air fryer basket after scraping it onto a 6" round baking dish.
4. Cook for 15 minutes, or until the mixture is bubbling and the top starts to brown. Serve hot.

GRILLED BELL PEPPERS

4 servings

Time to cook: 40 minutes.

Ingredients:

- 12 small bell peppers
- 1 small sweet onion
- 1 teaspoon Maggi sauce
- 1 tablespoon of extra virgin olive oil.

Directions:

1. Heat the olive oil and Maggi sauce in an air fryer set to 320°F.
2. Before adding the onion to the air fryer, peel it and cut it into 1-inch pieces.
3. Wash the peppers and remove the stems. Remove all the seeds by slicing them into 1-inch pieces and using water if required.
4. Add the peppers to the Air Fryer.
5. Bake for about 25 minutes, or until done. Serve immediately.

CHIPS MADE WITH KALE

2 servings

Time to cook: 5 minutes.

Ingredients:

- 4 medium kale leaves, about 1 ounce each.
- 2 tbsp. olive oil.
- Two teaspoons of soy sauce (regular or low-sodium) or gluten-free tamari
- Sauce

Directions:

1. Preheat the air fryer to 400 degrees F.
1. Separate the leaves from the stalks. Each leaf should be cut into three sections. Place them in a large mixing dish.
2. Combine the olive oil and soy or tamari sauce in a mixing bowl. To coat, toss thoroughly. To get the liquids to cling to the leaves, gently brush them down the edge of the bowl.
3. Once the machine has reached temperature, arrange the leaf pieces in a single layer in the basket. Air-fry for 5 minutes, tossing and rearranging once halfway through, or until the chips are dry and crispy. Keep an eye on them so they don't become dark brown around the edges.
4. Carefully transfer the contents of the basket to a wire rack. Allow at least 5 minutes to cool before serving. Uncovered on the rack, the chips may last up to 8 hours.

BEEF -PORK & LAMB RECIPES

PROVENÇAL GRILLED RIB-EYE

4 servings

Time to cook: 25 minutes.

Ingredients:

- 4 ribeye steaks
- 1 tbsp. Provence herbs
- Season with salt & pepper to taste.

Directions:

1. Preheat the air fryer to 360 degrees Fahrenheit. The herbs, salt, and pepper season the steaks. Cook for 8–12 minutes, turning once, in an oiled frying basket. Check for doneness with a thermometer and adjust the time as required. Allow the steak to rest for a few minutes before serving.

DOGS ON A STICK

Servings: 8

Time to cook: 7 minutes.

Ingredients:

- 8 hot dogs made with meat
- 8 buns for hot dogs

Directions:

1. Preheat the air fryer to 400 degrees F.
2. Cook the hot dogs for 7 minutes in the air fryer basket. Place one hot dog in each bun. Serve hot.

BEEF ROAST

Servings: 6

Time to cook: 60 minutes.

Ingredients:

- 1 roast beef top round
- 1 teaspoon coarse sea salt
- 1/2 teaspoons of black pepper, ground
- 1 teaspoon dried rosemary
- 1/2 tablespoon garlic powder
- 1 tablespoon coconut oil, melted

Directions:

1. Season both sides of the roast with salt, pepper, rosemary, and garlic powder. Drizzle with coconut oil to finish. Place the roast, fatty side down, in an ungreased air fryer basket. Preheat the oven to 3750F and set the timer for 60 minutes, flipping the roast halfway through. When no pink remains and the internal temperature is at least 180°F, the roast is done. Serve hot.

LAMB CHOPS WITH ROSEMARY

4 servings

Time to cook: 6 minutes.

Ingredients:

- 8 lamb loin chops.
- 1 tablespoon extra-virgin olive oil
- 1 teaspoon dried rosemary, crushed
- 2 minced garlic cloves.
- 1 teaspoon sea salt, coarse
- 1/4 tsp. black pepper

Directions:

1. Combine the lamb chops, olive oil, rosemary, garlic, salt, and pepper in a large mixing bowl. Allow for 10 minutes at room temperature.
2. In the meantime, preheat the air fryer to 380°F.
3. Cook the lamb chops for 3 minutes on one side, then 3 minutes on the other.

THESE CHEESEBURGERS ARE DELICIOUS

4 servings

Time to cook: 12 minutes.

Ingredients:

- 1 pound beef ground
- 4 slices of cheddar cheese.
- half tablespoon of Italian seasoning
- Pepper
- Salt
- Spray cooking oil on

Directions:

1. Lightly coat the air fryer basket with cooking spray.
2. In a mixing bowl, combine ground beef, Italian seasoning, pepper, and salt.
3. Shape the meat mixture into four equal patties and drop them into the air fryer basket.
4. Bake at 375°F for 5 minutes. Cook for 5 minutes longer on the opposite side of the patties.
5. Place cheese slices on top of each burger and cook for 2 minutes more.
6. Plate the dish and serve.

MEATBALLS FROM ITALY

8 servings

Time to cook: 12 minutes.

Ingredients:

- 3/4-pound ground beef
- 6 ounces of mild or spicy Italian sausage meat in bulk.
- 1/2 cups of seasoned dry Italian-style bread crumbs
- One large egg
- 3 tbsp milk (whole or low-fat)
- Spray with olive oil.

Directions:

1. Preheat the air fryer to 375°F.
2. In a mixing bowl, combine the ground beef, Italian sausage meat, bread crumbs, egg, and milk. Form this mixture into big meatballs with clean hands, using a 1/4-cup for each. Place the meatballs on a big chopping board and sprinkle them with olive oil spray on both sides. When turning them, be gentle. They're delicate.
3. Place them in the basket with as much room between them as feasible after the machine has reached its temperature. The crucial point is that they do not come into contact with each other, even if there is just a fraction of an inch between them. Air-fry

the meatballs for 12 minutes without stirring, or until a meat thermometer stuck into one of the meatballs reads 165°F.

4. Gently pick up the meatballs one at a time with kitchen tongs and place them on a chopping board or a serving dish. Allow for a few minutes of cooling before serving.

LAMB ROAST

Servings: 4

1 hour 30 minutes of cooking.

Ingredients:

- 2 1/2 lb. half lamb leg roast, cut into slices
- 2 garlic cloves cut into thin slivers
- 1 tablespoon dried rosemary
- 1 tablespoon olive oil (extra virgin)
- To taste, Himalayan rock salt & cracked peppercorns.

Directions:

1. Preheat the Air Fryer to 400 degrees Fahrenheit and spray an Air Fryer basket with cooking spray.
2. Fill the slits with garlic slithers and season with rosemary, olive oil, salt, and black pepper.
3. Place the lamb in the air fryer basket and cook for about 15 minutes.
4. Preheat the Air Fryer to 350°F and cook on the Roast setting for 1 hour and 15 minutes.
5. Plate the lamb chops and serve immediately.

BURGERS WITH BACON AND BLUE CHEESE

Servings: 4

Time to cook: 15 minutes.

Ingredients:

- 1 pound (70/30) ground beef
- 6 cooked sugar-free bacon pieces, coarsely chopped.
- 1/2 oz. blue cheese, crumbled
- 1/4 cups of yellow onion, peeled and chopped
- 1/2 teaspoons of salt
- 1/4 teaspoons of black pepper, ground

Directions:

1. In a large mixing bowl, combine the ground beef, bacon, blue cheese, and onion. Divide the mixture into four parts and form each portion into a Pitney. Season with salt and pepper to taste.

1. Place patties in a non-stick air fryer basket. Preheat the oven to 350°F and set the timer for 15 minutes, rotating the patties halfway through. When the interior temperature of the burger reaches 150°F for medium and 180°F for well, it is ready. Serve hot.

A BURGER WITH BACON AND BLUE CHEESE

Servings: 4

Time to cook: 15 minutes.

Ingredients:

- 1 pound ground sirloin
- 1/2 oz. blue cheese, crumbled
- 8 cooked and crumbled bacon slices.
- 1 tablespoon Worcestershire sauce
- 1 teaspoon coarse sea salt
- 1/2 teaspoons of black pepper, ground
- 4 pretzel buns
- Spray cooking oil on

Directions:

1. Preheat the air fryer to 370 degrees Fahrenheit.
2. Combine the sirloin, cheese, bacon, and Worcestershire sauce in a large mixing bowl.
3. Form the mixture into four patties and season each side with salt and pepper. Place it in the air fryer basket and coat with cooking spray.
4. Cook for 15 minutes, flipping halfway through, or until an internal temperature of 160°F is reached for well-done. To serve, place them on pretzel buns.

MEATLOAF

Servings: 4

Time to cook: 40 minutes.

Ingredients:

- 1 pound (80/20) lean ground beef
- 1 large egg
- 3 tablespoons Italian bread crumbs
- 1 teaspoon coarse sea salt
- 2 tbsp. of ketchup.

2 tbsp. brown sugar

Directions:

1. Preheat the air fryer to 350 degrees F.

2. In a large mixing bowl, combine the meat, egg, bread crumbs, and salt.
3. In a small bowl, combine ketchup and brown sugar.
4. Shape the meat mixture into a 6-inch-3-inch loaf and brush with the ketchup mixture.
5. Cook in the air fryer basket for 40 minutes, or until the internal temperature reaches at least 160°F. Serve hot.

GRILLED FIGS WITH PROSCIUTTO

Servings: 2

Cooking time: 8 minutes

Ingredients:

- 2 whole figs cut into quarters.
- 8 slices of prosciutto
- Season with pepper & salt to taste.

Directions:

1. Wrap a prosciutto slice around one fig slice and thread it onto a skewer. Repeat with the remaining ingredients. Place the skewer rack in the air fryer.
2. Bake at 390°F for 8 minutes. Turn the skewers halfway through the cooking period.
3. Arrange on plates and serve.

CHOPS OF LAMB

2 servings

Time to cook: 20 minutes.

Ingredients:

- 2 tablespoons olive oil
- 1/2 teaspoons of rosemary powder
- 1/2 teaspoon lemon juice
- 1 pound lamb chops, approximately 1 inch thick
- Pepper and salt.
- Sprayed frying oil.

Directions:

1. Combine the oil, rosemary, and lemon juice and massage it all over the lamb chops. Season with salt and pepper to taste.
2. For the best taste, cover the lamb chops and place them in the fridge for 20 minutes.
3. Spray the air fryer basket with non-stick spray and add the lamb chops.
4. Bake for 20 minutes at 360 °F. This will cook the chops to medium-rare. The meat will be moist but no longer pink. Cook for another minute or two for well-done chops. Stop cooking after around 12 minutes and check for doneness for rare chops.

POULTRY RECIPES

WINGS OF CHICKEN

4 servings

Time to cook: 55 minutes.

Ingredients:

- 1 pound boneless chicken wings
- 3/4 cup all-purpose flour
- 1 tablespoon of old bay seasoning.
- 4 tablespoons of butter.
- A couple of freshly squeezed lemons

Directions:

1. Combine the all-purpose flour and Old Bay seasoning in a mixing basin.
1. Toss the chicken wings in the mixture to thoroughly coat each one.
2. Preheat the air fryer to 375 degrees F.
3. Shake the wings to remove any extra flour before placing them in the air fryer. You may need to perform this in many batches to avoid overlap.
4. Cook for 30-40 minutes, stirring frequently, until the wings are thoroughly cooked and crispy.
5. Meanwhile, melt the butter in a frying pan over medium heat. Squeeze one or two lemons into the pan and add the juice. Combine thoroughly.
6. Serve the wings with the sauce on top.

TURKEY BREAST WITH HERB SEASONING

4 servings

Time to cook: 35 minutes.

Ingredients:

- 2lb turkey breast
- 1 teaspoon fresh sage, chopped
- 1 teaspoon fresh rosemary, chopped
- 1 teaspoon fresh thyme, chopped
- Pepper
- Salt

Directions:

1. Spray the air fryer basket lightly with cooking spray.
2. Combine sage, rosemary, and thyme in a small dish.
3. Season the turkey breast with pepper and salt before rubbing it with the herb mixture.
4. Place the turkey breast in the air fryer basket and cook at 390 °F for 30-35 minutes.
5. Cut into slices before serving.

CHICKEN BREASTS WITH SWEET NUTTY SAUCE

Servings: 4

Time to cook: 30 minutes.

Ingredients:

- 2 chicken breasts cut in half lengthwise.
- 1/4 cups of honey mustard
- 1/4 cups of pecans, chopped
- 1 tablespoon extra-virgin olive oil
- 1 tbsp. chopped parsley

Directions:

1. Preheat the air fryer to 350 degrees Fahrenheit. Brush both sides of the chicken breasts with honey mustard and olive oil. In a bowl, combine the pecans. Coat the chicken breasts with the mixture. Air fried the breasts for 25 minutes, flipping once, in a greased frying basket. Allow for a 5-minute cool on a serving platter. Garnish with parsley and serve.

NACHOS WITH BAKED CHICKEN

Servings: 4

Time to cook: 7 minutes.

Ingredients:

- 50 tortilla chips
- 2 cups split cooked shredded chicken breast
- 2 cups Mexican-style shredded cheese, divided
- 1/2 cup pickled jalapeo peppers, sliced
- 1/2 cups of red onion, split

Directions:

1. Preheat the air fryer to 300 degrees F.
2. Cut a bowl out of foil to suit the form of the air fryer basket. Half of the tortilla chips should go in the bottom of the foil bowl, followed by 1 cup chicken, 1 cup cheese, 1/4 cups jalapeo, and 1/4 cups onion. Continue with the remaining chips and toppings.
2. Place the foil dish in the air fryer basket and cook for 7 minutes, or until the cheese melts and the toppings are cooked through. Serve hot.

THE FINEST GRILLED CHICKEN BREAST

2 servings

Time to cook: 12 minutes.

Ingredients:

- 2 skinless and boneless chicken breasts.
- 2 tablespoons of olive oil.
- Pepper
- Salt

Directions:

1. Replace the air fryer basket with the air fryer grill pan.
2. Arrange the chicken breasts in a single layer on the grill pan. Season the chicken with salt and pepper. Drizzle with olive oil.
3. Bake the chicken for 12 minutes at 375 degrees Fahrenheit.
4. Plate the dish and serve.

CHICKEN THIGHS WITH CINNAMON

4 servings

Time to cook: 30 minutes.

Ingredients:

- 2 pounds chicken thighs
- A sprinkle of black pepper and salt.
- 2 tbsp of olive oil.
- 1/2 teaspoons cinnamon powder

Directions:

1. Season the chicken thighs with salt and pepper before rubbing with the other ingredients. Place the chicken thighs in the air fryer basket and cook for 15 minutes on each side at 360°F. Divide it into plates and serve.

PARTRIDGE, ROSEMARY

4 servings

Time to cook: 14 minutes.

Ingredients:

- 10 oz. partridges
- 1 teaspoon dried rosemary
- 1 tbsp. melted butter
- 1 teaspoon coarse sea salt

Directions:

1. Season the partridge halves with salt and dry rosemary. After that, brush them with melted butter. Preheat the air fryer to 385 degrees Fahrenheit. Cook the partridge halves in the air fryer for 8 minutes. Cook for another 6 minutes after flipping the poultry.

CRISPY & EASY CHICKEN WINGS

8 servings

Time to cook: 20 minutes.

Ingredients:

- 1 pound and a half of chicken wings
- 2 tablespoons of olive oil.
- Pepper
- Salt

Directions:

1. Oil the chicken wings and place them in the air fryer basket.
2. Bake chicken wings at 370°F for 15 minutes.
3. Shake the basket and cook for another 5 minutes at 400 degrees Fahrenheit.
4. Season the chicken wings with salt and pepper to taste.
5. Arrange on plates and serve.

CHICKEN BREASTS (BASIC)

Servings: 4

Time to cook: 15 minutes.

Ingredients:

- 2 tablespoons of olive oil.
- Two breasts of chicken
- Season with salt & pepper to taste.
- 1/2 teaspoons of garlic powder
- 1/2 teaspoons of rosemary

Directions:

1. Preheat the air fryer to 350 degrees Fahrenheit. Rub olive oil over the tops and bottoms of the chicken breasts, then season with garlic powder, rosemary, salt, and pepper. Air cooks the chicken in the frying basket for 9 minutes, turning once. Allow it to rest for 5 minutes on a serving platter before cutting into cubes. Serving and having fun

SANDWICHES WITH BUFFALO CHICKEN

Servings: 4

Time to cook: 20 minutes.

Ingredients:

- 4 chicken thighs, skinless and boneless
- 1 tablespoon dried ranch seasoning
- 1/4-cup hot sauce
- 4 pepper jack cheese slices.
- 4 sandwich buns

Directions:

1. Preheat the air fryer to 375 degrees F.
2. Coat each chicken thigh in cooking spray and season with ranch seasoning.
3. Cook for 20 minutes, flipping halfway through, until the chicken is brown around the edges and the internal temperature reaches 165°F.
4. To serve, drizzle buffalo sauce over the chicken, top with a piece of cheese, and arrange on buns.

CHICKEN WITH CREAMY ONION SAUCE

Servings: 4

Time to cook: 20 minutes.

Ingredients:

- 1 ½ cup of onion soup mix
- 1 gallon mushroom soup
- Half cup of heavy cream

Directions:

1. Preheat the fryer to 400 degrees Fahrenheit. In a frying pan, combine the mushrooms, onion mixture, and cream. Heat for 1 minute on low heat. Allow the heated mixture to remain for 25 minutes on top of the chicken pieces. Cook the marinated chicken for 15 minutes in the air fryer cooking basket. With the remaining cream, serve.

QUICK CHICKEN FILLING

2 servings

Time to cook: 8 minutes.

Ingredients:

- 1 pound chicken tenders, skinless and boneless
- 1/2 teaspoons of cumin powder
- 1/2 tablespoon garlic powder
- Sprayed frying oil.

Directions:

1. Sprinkle salt and pepper on raw chicken tenders.
2. To prevent sticking, lightly coat the air fryer basket with cooking spray.
2. Arrange the chicken in a single layer in the air fryer basket.
3. Cook the chicken strips for 4 minutes at 390°F, then flip and cook for another 4 minutes.
4. Check for completion. Thick tenders may need an extra minute or two.

CHICKEN BREAST WITH LEMON PEPPER

Servings: 1

Time to Cook:

Ingredients:

- 1 pound breast of chicken
- 1 tsp. minced garlic
- 2 lemons, rinds and juice saved
- Season with salt & pepper to taste.

Directions:

1. Preheat the air fryer.
2. In an air fryer-safe baking dish, combine all of the ingredients.
1. Place the air fryer basket in the air fryer.
3. Bake at 400°F for 20 minutes, covered.

CHICKEN AND BACON WRAPPED

6 servings

Time to cook: 20 minutes.

Ingredients:

- 1 chicken breast, cut into 6 pieces
- 6 rashers of back bacon
- 1 soft cheese tablespoon

Directions:

4. Place the bacon rashers on a flat surface and spread the soft cheese on one side.
5. Place a slice of chicken on each bacon rasher. Wrap the bacon around the chicken and secure it with a toothpick stick. Place them in the air fryer basket.
2. Air fry at 350°F for 15 minutes.

TERIYAKI CHICKEN LEGS

2 servings

Time to cook: 20 minutes.

Ingredients:

- Teriyaki sauce (four tablespoons)
- 1 teaspoon of orange juice.
- 1 teaspoon smoked paprika
- 4 thighs of chicken
- Sprayed frying oil.

Directions:

1. Combine the teriyaki sauce, orange juice, and smoked paprika in a mixing bowl. Brush the chicken legs on both sides.
2. Coat the air fryer basket with non-stick cooking spray before adding the chicken.
3. Bake at 360°F for 6 minutes. Turnover and baste with the sauce. Cook for 6 minutes longer, then flip and baste. Cook for another 8 minutes, or until the juices flow clear when the chicken is probed with a fork.

CHICKEN WINGS WITH BUFFALO SAUCE

3 servings

Time to cook: 37 minutes.

Ingredients:

- Chicken wings weighing 2 pounds
- 1 teaspoon sea salt
- 1/4 teaspoons of black pepper
- 1 tbsp. buffalo sauce

Directions:

1. Using clean kitchen towels wash and dry the chicken wings.
1. Toss the chicken wings in a large mixing dish with salt and pepper.
2. Preheat the air fryer to 380 degrees F.
3. Place the wings in the fryer and cook for 15 minutes, stirring every now and then.
4. Put the wings in a mixing dish. Toss with the buffalo sauce until evenly coated.
5. Return the chicken to the air fryer and cook for 5-6 minutes more.

TURKEY NUGGETS WITH THYME

Servings: 2

Time to cook: 20 minutes.

Ingredients:

- 1 egg, beaten
- One cup of breadcrumbs
- 1 tablespoon thyme dried
- 1/2 tablespoons of dried parsley
- Season with salt & pepper to taste.

Directions:

1. Preheat the air fryer to 350 degrees Fahrenheit. Combine the ground chicken, thyme, parsley, salt, and pepper in a mixing bowl. Form the mixture into little balls. Dip in the breadcrumbs, then the egg, and finally back in the breadcrumbs. Spray the air fryer basket with cooking spray and cook the nuggets for 10 minutes, shaking once.

SCALLOPS WITH A SWEET-AND-SPICY CURE

Servings: 3

Time to cook: 5 minutes.

Ingredients:

- Thai sweet chilli sauce, 6 tbsp
- 2 cups crushed Rice Kris pies or other rice-puffed cereal
- 2 tsp yellow curry powder (store-bought or homemade).
- 1 pound sea scallops
- Vegetable oil spray

Directions:

1. Preheat the air fryer to 400 degrees F.
2. Arrange two shallow soup plates or tiny pie plates on your counter, one for the chilli sauce and the other for the curry-flavored crumbs.
3. Coat each scallop on both sides with the chilli sauce. Place it in the cereal mixture and flip it to coat it evenly. Shake any excess off the scallop and place it on a cutting board. Dip and coat the remaining scallops as needed. Spray all sides with the vegetable oil spray.
4. Arrange the scallops in the basket with as much air space as possible between them. Allow for 5 minutes of air-frying, or until lightly browned and crispy.
2. Take out the basket. Set aside for 2 minutes to allow the coating to harden. Then, place the contents of the basket on a dish and serve immediately.

SEA BASS WITH LEMON AND THYME

3 servings

Time to cook: 15 minutes.

Ingredients:

- Trimmed and peeled sea bass, 8 oz.
- 4 lemon wedges.
- 1 teaspoon fresh thyme
- 2 tbsp. sesame oil.
- 1 teaspoon coarse sea salt

Directions:

1. Rub the sea bass with thyme, salt, and sesame oil after stuffing it with lemon slices. Preheat the air fryer to 385°F, and then place the fish in the air fryer basket. 12 minutes in the oven then turn the fish over and cook for another 3 minutes.

SALMON WITH MAPLE BUTTER

Servings: 4

Time to cook: 12 minutes.

Ingredients:

- 2 tsp salted butter, melted
- 1 teaspoon low-carb maple syrup
- 1 teaspoon yellow mustard
- 4 fillets of boneless, skinless salmon.
- 1/2 teaspoons of salt

Directions:

1. In a small mixing dish, combine the butter, syrup, and mustard. Brush 1/2 of the mixture on both sides of each fillet. Season both sides of the fillets with salt. Place the fish in an unoiled air fryer basket. Preheat the oven to 400°F and set the timer for 12 minutes. Brush both sides of the fillets with the remaining syrup mixture halfway through cooking. When done, the salmon will flake easily and have an internal temperature of at least 145°F. Serve hot.

QUICK AND EASY LIME-GARLIC SHRIMP

Servings: 1

Time to cook: 6 minutes.

Ingredients:

- 1 garlic clove, minced
- 1 pound fresh shrimp
- 1 lime, juiced and zested
- Season with salt & pepper to taste.

Directions:

1. In a mixing bowl, whisk together all of the ingredients.
2. Preheat the air fryer to 390 degrees F.
3. Skewer the shrimp with the metal skewers that came with the two-tier rack accessories.
4. Cook on the top rack for 6 minutes.

CAPERS AND TOMATOES WITH SWORDFISH

2 servings

Time to cook: 10 minutes.

Ingredients:

1. 2 swordfish steaks, 1 inch thick.
2. A sprinkle of black pepper and salt.
3. 30 ounces diced tomatoes
4. 2 tablespoons capers, drained
5. 1 tablespoon red wine, 1 tablespoon vinegar
6. 2 tsp oregano, chopped

Directions:

1. In an air fryer-compatible pan, combine all of the ingredients, stir, and cook at 390°F for 10 minutes, turning the fish halfway through. Serve the mixture on individual plates.

SCALLOPS WITH GARLIC AND LEMON

Servings: 2

Time to cook: 15 minutes.

Ingredients:

- 2 tablespoons melted butter
- 1 garlic clove, minced
- 1 teaspoon of lemon juice
- 1 pound of massive sea scallops

Directions:

1. Preheat the air fryer to 400 degrees Fahrenheit. In a mixing dish, combine the butter, garlic, and lemon juice. Coat the scallops with the mixture on both sides. Air fried the scallops in the frying basket for 4 minutes, turning once. Cook for 4 minutes longer, turning once, after brushing the tops of each scallop with the butter mixture. Serving and having fun

FLOUNDER CUTLETS IN RESTAURANT STYLE

2 servings

Time to cook: 15 minutes.

Ingredients:

1. 1 egg
2. 1 cup Pecorino Romano shredded
3. To taste, season with sea salt & white pepper.
4. Cayenne pepper, 1/2 teaspoon
5. 1 teaspoon dried parsley flakes
6. 2 flounder fillets

Directions:

1. To prepare the breading station, whisk the egg until it is foamy.
2. In a separate bowl, combine the Pecorino Romano cheese and seasonings.
3. Dredge the fish in the cracker crumb mixture, rotating a number of times to coat it evenly, after dipping it in the egg mixture.
4. Cook for 5 minutes in a 390°F preheated air fryer before flipping and cooking for another 5 minutes. Enjoy!

STICKS OF FISH

4 servings

Time to cook: 20 minutes.

Ingredients:

- 1 pound sliced tilapia fillets
- 1 large beaten egg
- 2 tsp. Old Bay seasoning
- 1 tablespoon extra-virgin olive oil
- 1 cup healthy bread crumbs

Directions:

1. Preheat the air fryer to 400 degrees F.
2. In a small dish, combine the bread crumbs, Old Bay, and oil. In a small dish, place the egg.
3. Dredge the fish sticks in the egg with a fork. Place them in the fryer's basket and coat them with bread crumbs.
4. Cook for 10 minutes, or until the fish is golden brown.
5. Serve right away.

QUICK AND SIMPLE SHRIMP

Servings: 2

Time to cook: 5 minutes.

Ingredients:

- Tiger shrimp weigh 1/2 pounds.
- 1 tablespoon olive oil (extra virgin)
- 1/2 tsp. old bay seasoning
- 1/4 tsp. smoked paprika
- 1/4 tsp. cayenne pepper
- Season with salt to taste.

Directions:

1. Preheat the Air Fryer to 390 degrees Fahrenheit and spray an Air Fryer basket with cooking spray.
2. In a large mixing basin, blend all of the ingredients until they are thoroughly incorporated.
3. Cook the shrimp in the air fryer basket for about 5 minutes.
4. Remove from the oven and serve immediately.

CAJUN LOBSTER TAILS

Servings: 4

Time to cook: 10 minutes.

Ingredients:

- Four lobster tails
- 2 tsp salted butter, melted
- 2 tablespoons lemon juice
- 1 tablespoon Cajun seasoning

Directions:

1. Preheat the air fryer to 400 degrees F.
2. Using kitchen scissors carefully cut apart the lobster tails and peels back the shell slightly to reveal the flesh. Drizzle each tail with butter and lemon juice, then season with Cajun spice.
3. Cook the lobster tails in the air fryer basket for 10 minutes, or until the shells are bright red and the interior temperature reaches 145°F.Serve hot.

HADDOCK WITH HERBS

Servings: 2

Time to cook: 8 minutes.

Ingredients:

- 2 fillets of haddock,
- 2 tablespoons pine nuts
- 3 tablespoons fresh basil, chopped
- 1 tbsp. grated Parmesan cheese
- 1/2 cup extra virgin olive oil
- To taste, season with salt and black pepper.

Directions:

1. Preheat the Air Fryer to 355°F and coat a cooking spray-coated Air Fryer basket.
2. Season the haddock fillets with salt and black pepper, and then drizzle with olive oil evenly.
3. Cook the haddock fillets for 8 minutes in the air fryer basket.
4. Arrange the haddock fillets on individual serving dishes.
5. Meanwhile, in a food processor, combine the other ingredients and pulse until smooth.
6. Pour the cheese sauce over the haddock fillets and serve immediately.

FILLETS OF FRIED CATFISH

Servings: 2

Time to cook: 40 minutes.

Ingredients:

- 3 tablespoons of breadcrumbs.
- 1 tbsp. cayenne pepper
- 1 teaspoon seasoned dried fish
- 2 chopped parsley sprigs.
- Optional salt to taste
- Spray cooking oil on

Directions:

1. Preheat the air fryer to 400 degrees Fahrenheit. In a zipper bag, combine all of the dry ingredients except the parsley. Pat the fish pieces dry before adding them. Close the bag and shake vigorously to thoroughly coat the fish. Do this with one piece of fish at a time.

2. Spray the fish lightly with olive oil. Place them in the frying basket one at a time, depending on their size. Cook for 10 minutes with the air fryer closed. Cook for another 10 minutes after flipping the fish. Cook for 3 minutes longer for added crispiness. Garnish with parsley and serve.

BAKED COD IN ITALIAN SAUCE

Servings: 4

Time to cook: 12 minutes.

Ingredients:

- 4 fillets of cod.
- 2 tsp salted butter, melted
- 1 tablespoon of Italian seasoning.
- 1/4 teaspoons of salt
- 1/2 cup marinara sauce (low carb)

Directions:

1. Place the fish in a 6" round non-stick baking dish that has not been oiled. Pour butter over the fish and season with salt and Italian spice. Marinara sauce on top

2. Insert the dish into the air fryer basket. Preheat the oven to 350°F and set the timer for 12 minutes. When done, the fillets will be lightly browned, flaky, and have an internal temperature of at least 145°F. Serve hot.

INCREDIBLE CRISPY FRIED SALMON SKIN

Servings: 4

Time to cook: 10 minutes.

Ingredients:

- 1/2 lb. salmon skin, dried
- Four tablespoons coconut oil
- Season with salt and pepper to taste.

Directions:

1. Before using the air fryer, preheat it for 5 minutes.
2. In a large mixing bowl, thoroughly combine everything.
3. Transfer to the frying basket and cover with a lid.
4. Bake for 10 minutes at 400 °F.
5. Shake the pan halfway during the cooking time to evenly fry the skin.

SIMPLE LOBSTER TAIL WITH BUTTER

Servings: 4

Time to cook: 6 minutes.

Ingredients:

- 2 tbsp. softened butter.
- Four lobster tails.
- Season with salt & pepper to taste.

Directions:

1. Preheat the air fryer to 390 degrees F.
2. Set the grill pan attachment in place.
3. Using a pair of kitchen scissors, cut the lobster through the tail portion.
4. Brush the lobster tails with melted butter and season to taste with salt and pepper.
5. Grill on the grill pan for 6 minutes.

SALMON FILLETS WITH LEMON ROASTING

Servings: 3

Time to cook: 7 minutes.

Ingredients:

- Three skin-on 6-ounce salmon fillets
- Spray with olive oil.
- 9 thinly sliced lemons.
- 3/4 teaspoons of black pepper, ground
- 1/4 tsp. table salt

Directions:

1. Preheat the air fryer to 400 degrees F.
2. Liberally spray each fillet's skin with olive oil spray. Place the fillets on your work area, skin side down. Place three lemon slices overlapping along the length of each salmon fillet. Season with pepper and salt to taste. Light coat with olive oil spray.
3. Transfer the fillets to the basket one at a time, keeping as much air space between them as possible, using a non-stick spatula. Uninterrupted air-fry for 7 minutes, or until cooked through.
4. Transfer the fillets to serving dishes using a non-stick spatula. Allow it to cool for a minute or two before serving.

BURGERS WITH SHRIMP

Servings: 4

Time to cook: 10 minutes.

Ingredients:

- 10 ounces peeled and deveined medium shrimp
- 1/4 cups of mayonnaise
- 1/2 cups of bread crumbs (panko)
- 1/2 tsp. Old Bay Seasoning
- 1/4 teaspoons of salt
- /18 tsp. ground black pepper
- 4 hamburger buns

Directions:

1. Preheat the air fryer to 400 degrees F.
2. In a food processor, pulse the shrimp four times until broken down.
3. Combine the shrimp, mayonnaise, bread crumbs, Old Bay, salt, and pepper in a large mixing dish. 4.
4. Divide the ingredients into four equal halves and shape them into patties. They will feel damp but should retain their form.

5. Place the burgers in the air fryer basket and cook for 10 minutes, flipping halfway, until golden and the internal temperature reaches 145°F. Served on heated buns.

NUGGETS OF COD

Servings: 4

Time to cook: 12 minutes.

Ingredients:

- 2 cod fillets, boneless and skinless.
- 1 1/2 teaspoons of salt (divided)
- 3/4 teaspoons of black pepper, split
- Two huge eggs
- 1 cup bread crumbs, unbleached

Directions:

1. Preheat the air fryer to 350 degrees F.
2. Cut the fillets of fish into sixteen equal pieces. Season the fish nuggets in a large mixing bowl with 1 teaspoon salt and 1/2 teaspoon pepper.
3. Whisk the eggs in a separate dish. In a separate small dish, combine the bread crumbs with the remaining 1/2 teaspoons of salt and 1/4 teaspoons of pepper.
4. Dip the nuggets in the eggs one at a time, brushing off any excess before rolling in the bread crumb mixture. Repeat until you have a total of sixteen nuggets.
5. Spray the nuggets with cooking spray and place them in the air fryer basket. Cook for 12 minutes, stirring halfway through. When the nuggets are golden brown and have an interior temperature of at least 145°F, they are done. Serve hot.

FILLETS OF TILAPIA

2 servings

Time to cook: 7 minutes.

Ingredients:

- Two fillets of tilapia
- 1 teaspoon of old bay seasoning
- Half teaspoon of butter
- 1/4 teaspoons of lemon pepper
- Pepper
- Salt

Directions:

1. Lightly coat the air fryer basket with cooking spray. 2.
2. Season the fish fillets in the air fryer basket with lemon pepper, old bay seasoning, pepper, and salt.
3. Coat fish fillets with cooking spray and bake at 400 °F for 7 minutes.
4. Serve and enjoy

CAJUN SCALLOPS WRAPPED IN BACON

Servings: 4

Time to cook: 13 minutes.

Ingredients:

- 8 slices bacon
- 8 washed and dried sea scallops
- 1 teaspoon Cajun seasoning
- 4 teaspoons of melted salted butter

Directions:

1. Preheat the air fryer to 375 degrees F.
2. Cook the bacon in the air fryer basket for 3 minutes. Remove the bacon and wrap one piece around each scallop before securing with a toothpick.
3. Sprinkle the Cajun spice evenly over the scallops. Spritz scallops gently with cooking spray and arrange them in a single layer in the air fryer basket. Then cook for 10 minutes, flipping halfway through, until the scallops are opaque and hard and the internal temperature reaches at least 130°F. Drizzle with melted butter. Serve hot.

Vegetarians Recipes

Wings with almond flour batter

Servings: 4

Time to cook: 25 minutes.

Ingredients:

- 1/4 cups of melted butter
- One-quarter cup almond flour
- 16 chicken wing pieces
- 2 tablespoons powdered stevia
- 4 teaspoons minced garlic
- Season with salt & pepper to taste.

Directions:

1. Before using the air fryer, preheat it for 5 minutes.
2. Combine the chicken wings, almond flour, stevia powder, and garlic in a mixing bowl. Season to taste with salt & pepper.
3. Place in the air fryer basket and cook for 25 minutes at 400 °F.
4. Give the fryer basket a good shake halfway through the cooking time.
5. Once done, place in a bowl and top with melted butter. To coat, toss everything together.

1 CUP BELL PEPPERS

Servings: 4

Time to cook: 8 minutes.

Ingredients:

- 8 tiny red bell peppers, removing the tops and seeds.
- 1 teaspoon fresh parsley, chopped
- 3/4 cups of crumbled feta cheese
- 1/2 teaspoons of olive oil
- To taste, freshly ground black pepper.

Directions:

1. Preheat the Air Fryer to 390 degrees Fahrenheit and spray an Air Fryer basket with cooking spray.
2. In a mixing dish, combine the feta cheese, parsley, olive oil, and black pepper.
3. Fill the bell peppers with the feta cheese mixture and place them in the air fryer basket.
4. Allow to cook for 8 minutes before serving.

GOURMET WASABI POPCORN

2 servings

Time to cook: 30 minutes.

Ingredients:

- Half teaspoon of brown sugar
- 1 teaspoon coarse sea salt
- 1/2 teaspoon wasabi powder, sifted
- 1 tbsp avocado oil
- 3 tablespoons popcorn kernels

Directions:

1. Toss the dry corn kernels with the other ingredients in the Air Fryer basket.
2. Bake at 395°F for 15 minutes, shaking the basket every 5 minutes. Working in two groups
3. Taste, adjust seasonings, and serve immediately. Good appetite!

ROASTED SPAGHETTI SQUASH

Servings: 6

45-minute cooking time

Ingredients:

- 1 peeled and halved spaghetti squash
- 2 tbsp of coconut oil.
- 4 teaspoons of melted salted butter
- 1 teaspoon garlic powder
- 2 tablespoons of parsley, dried

Directions:

1. Brush the spaghetti squash shell with coconut oil. Buttered the inside of the pan. Garlic powder and parsley should be sprinkled throughout.
2. Place the squash, skin side up, in an ungreased air fryer basket, working in batches if necessary. Set the oven temperature to 350°F and the timer for 30 minutes. When the timer goes off, rotate the squash and cook for another 15 minutes, or until fork-tender.
3. Using a fork, remove the spaghetti strands from the shell and serve warm.

GREEN BEANS WITH LEMON

Servings: 3

Time to cook: 12 minutes.

Ingredients:

- 1 pound green beans, trimmed and halved
- 1 tsp. melted butter
- 1 tbsp lemon juice, freshly squeezed
- 1/4 tsp. garlic powder

Directions:

1. Preheat the Air Fryer to 400 degrees Fahrenheit and spray an Air Fryer basket with cooking spray.
2. Toss all of the ingredients in a mixing bowl to coat well.
3. Place the green beans in the air fryer basket and cook for 12 minutes.
4. Transfer to a serving platter and serve hot.

WITH OLIVES, BROCCOLI

Servings: 4

Time to cook: 19 minutes.

Ingredients:

- 2 pounds of broccoli, stems and florets chopped into 1-inch pieces.
- 1/3 cup Kalamata olives, halved and pitted
- 1/4 cups of grated Parmesan cheese
- 2 tbsp of olive oil.
- As needed, season with salt and black pepper.
- 2 teaspoons freshly grated lemon zest

Directions:

1. Preheat the Air Fryer to 400 degrees Fahrenheit and spray an Air Fryer basket with cooking spray.
2. Boil the broccoli for 4 minutes, and then drain thoroughly.
3. In a mixing bowl, toss broccoli with oil, salt, and black pepper to coat thoroughly.
4. Place the broccoli in the air fryer basket and cook for about 15 minutes.
5. Stir in the olives, lemon zest, and cheese before serving.

CAULIFLOWER WITH BROCCOLI

Servings: 4

Time to cook: 20 minutes.

Ingredients:

- 1 1/2 cups of broccoli, sliced into 1-inch cubes.
- 1 1/2 cups of cauliflower, chopped into 1-inch chunks.
- 1 tablespoon olive oil (extra virgin)
- Salt as needed

Directions:

1. Preheat the Air Fryer to 375°F and coat a cooking spray-coated Air Fryer basket.
2. Toss the vegetables with the olive oil and salt in a mixing bowl to coat thoroughly.
3. Place the vegetable mixture in the air fryer basket and cook for 20 minutes, stirring once during the cooking time.
4. Place it in a dish and serve it hot.

BROCCOLI SALAD

Servings: 2

Cooking time is 15 minutes.

Ingredients:

- 3 cups of broccoli florets those are fresh.
- 2 tbsp. coconut oil, melted
- 1/4 cups chopped
- 1/2 large lemons, juiced

Directions:

1. Fill a baking dish measuring six inches with broccoli florets. Pour the coconut oil that has been melted over the broccoli and add the salt. Blend together. Place the dish into an air fryer.
2. Cook at 380 degrees Fahrenheit for seven minutes, stirring halfway through.
3. Place the broccoli in a bowl and sprinkle it with the lemon juice.

AVOCADO WRAPS

Servings: 5

Time to cook: 15 minutes.

Ingredients:

- 10 wrappers for egg rolls
- 1 tomato, diced
- 1/4 teaspoon black pepper
- half teaspoon of salt

Directions:

1. In a mixing basin, mash all of the filling ingredients with a fork until reasonably smooth. There should still be some pieces remaining. Divide the emotions among the egg wraps. Brush your finger around the edges to help the wrappers close properly. The wrappers should be rolled and sealed.
2. Place them in the air fryer on a baking sheet lined dish. Cook for 5 minutes at 350°F. Enjoy with a sweet chilli dipping sauce.

AIR FRYER SKEWERED CORN

Servings: 2

Time to cook: 25 minutes.

Ingredients:

- 1 pound apricot halves
- 2 cobs of corn.
- 2 medium green peppers peeled and diced.
- 2 tsp. prepared mustard.
- Season with salt & pepper to taste.

Directions:

1. Preheat the air fryer to 330 degrees F.
2. Insert the air fryer's grill pan attachment.
3. Using the skewer accessories, skewer the corn, green peppers, and apricots on the double-layer rack. Season to taste with salt and pepper.
4. Cook the skewered corn for 25 minutes on the two-layer rack.
5. Once completed, brush with prepared mustard.

GREEN BEANS FROM THE GARDEN

Servings: 4

Time to cook: 12 minutes.

Ingredients:

- 1 pound green beans, cleaned and trimmed
- 1 tsp. melted butter
- 1 tbsp lemon juice, freshly squeezed
- 1/4 tsp. garlic powder
- To taste, season with salt & freshly ground pepper.

Directions:

1. Preheat the Air Fryer to 400 degrees Fahrenheit and spray an Air Fryer basket with cooking spray.
2. In a large mixing bowl, combine all of the ingredients and transfer to the air fryer basket.
3. Cook for 8 minutes before transferring to a bowl.

APPLE-LICIOUS APPLE CHIPS

Servings: 1

Time to cook: 6 minutes.

Ingredients:

- 1/2 teaspoons of cumin powder
- 1 cored and thinly sliced apple
- 1 tablespoon sugar
- A grain of salt

Directions:

1. Toss all of the ingredients in a mixing bowl to coat.
2. Place the cut apples on the grill pan attachment and place it in the air fryer.
3. Close the air fryer and cook for 6 minutes at 390 °F.

VEGETABLE SIDE DISHES RECIPES

CHILLI OIL BRUSSELS SPROUTS

4 servings

Time to cook: 30 minutes.

Ingredients:

- 1 cup Brussels sprouts, quartered
- 1 tablespoon extra-virgin olive oil
- 1 tsp. chilli oil
- Season with salt & pepper to taste.

Directions:

1. Preheat the air fryer to 350 degrees Fahrenheit. In a bowl, toss the Brussels sprouts with olive oil, Chile oil, salt, and black pepper. Place it in the frying basket. Bake for 20 minutes, tossing the basket several times while cooking, or until the sprouts are crispy on the exterior and juicy on the inside. Serving and having fun

ROASTED BRUSSELS SPROUTS

Servings: 6

Time to cook: 10 minutes.

Ingredients:

- 1 pound fresh Brussels sprouts, trimmed and halved
- 2 tbsp of coconut oil.
- 1/2 teaspoons of salt
- 1/4 teaspoons of black pepper, ground
- 1/2 tablespoon garlic powder
- 1 tablespoon salted butter, melted

Directions:

1. Place the Brussels sprouts in a large mixing basin. Sprinkle with salt, pepper, and garlic powder and drizzle with coconut oil.
2. Place Brussels sprouts in an air fryer basket that has not been oiled. Set the timer for 10 minutes and adjust the temperature to 350°F, shaking the basket three times throughout cooking. When done, the Brussels sprouts will be dark golden and soft.
3. Toss cooked sprouts in a wide serving dish with butter. Serve hot.

ASPARAGUS

4 servings

Time to cook: 9 minutes.

Ingredients:

- 1 bunch asparagus, cleaned and trimmed
- 1/8 teaspoons of crumbled dried tarragon
- Pepper and salt.
- 1–2 tbsp extra-light olive oil

Directions:

1. Arrange asparagus spears on a baking sheet or cutting board.
2. Season to taste with tarragon, salt, and pepper.
3. Drizzle with 1 teaspoon of oil and roll or mix the spears by hand. If necessary, add up to 1 teaspoon of additional oil and stir until all spears are gently coated.
4. Put the spears in the air fryer basket. Bend the longer spears if required to make them fit. It makes no difference if they don't lie flat.
5. Cook at 390°F for 5 minutes. Shake the basket or use a spoon to swirl the spears.
6. Cook for another 4 minutes, or until crispy-tender.

FRIES WITH PARMESAN AND GARLIC

4 servings

Time to cook: 20 minutes.

Ingredients:

- 2 medium washed Yukon gold potatoes
- 1 tablespoon extra-virgin olive oil
- 1 garlic clove, minced
- 2 tbsp finely grated parmesan cheese
- 1/4 teaspoon black pepper
- 1/4 teaspoons of salt
- 1 tablespoon freshly chopped parsley

Directions:

1. Preheat the air fryer to 400 degrees F.
2. Cut the potatoes into long, ¼ inch-thick strips. Toss the potatoes with the olive oil, garlic, cheese, pepper, and salt in a large mixing basin.
3. Cook for 4 minutes, shaking the basket halfway through, in the air fryer basket.
4. Remove from the oven and serve immediately.

CARROTS WITH A SAVOURY ROAST

Servings: 4

Time to cook: 12 minutes.

Ingredients:

- Baby carrots, 1 pound
- 2 tbsp. dry ranch seasoning.
- 3 tablespoons of melted salted butter.

Directions:

1. Preheat the air fryer to 360°F (180°C).
2. Arrange the carrots in a 6" round baking dish. Drizzle butter over carrots and season with ranch dressing. Gently toss to coat.
3. Place the carrots in the air fryer basket and cook for 12 minutes, stirring twice during the cooking time, or until soft. Serve hot.

ROASTED SWEET POTATOES MADE EASY

2 servings

45-minute cooking time.

Ingredients:

- 2 sweet potatoes, 10 to 12 oz (es)

Directions:

1. Preheat the air fryer to 350 degrees F.
2. Using the tines of a flatware fork, prick the sweet potatoes in four or five distinct places.
3. When the machine is ready, place the sweet potato (es) in the basket with as much air space as possible between them. Allow to air-fry for 45 minutes, or until fork pierced tender.
4. Transfer the sweet potatoes (es) to a wire rack using kitchen tongs. Allow it to cool for 5 minutes before serving.

BUTTERNUT SQUASH FRIES ON A BUDGET

3 servings

Time to cook: 16 minutes.

Ingredients:

- Spiralized butternut squash strands weigh 1 pound, 2 ounces.
- Spray with vegetable oil.
- Coarse sea salt or kosher salt to taste

Directions:

1. Preheat the air fryer to 375 degrees F.
2. Put the spiralized squash in a large mixing dish. Coat the strands with vegetable oil spray, toss well, coat again, and toss many times to ensure that all of the strands are greased.
3. When the machine is ready, pour the strands into the basket and spread them out into an equal layer. Air-fry the strands for 16 minutes, turning and rotating them every 4 minutes, or until lightly browned and crisp.
4. Transfer the contents of the basket to a serving dish, season with salt, and mix well before serving hot.

FRIES MADE WITH SWEET POTATOES

3 servings

Time to cook: 20 minutes

Ingredients:

- 2 sweet potatoes, 10 oz. (es)
- Spray with vegetable oil.
- Coarse sea salt or kosher salt to taste

Directions:

1. Preheat the air fryer to 400 degrees F.
2. Peel and cut the sweet potato (es) into 1/4-inch-thick slices lengthwise. Cut these slices into 1/4-inch-thick matchsticks by cutting them lengthwise. Coat these matchsticks with vegetable oil spray and place them in a basin. Toss them well, then spray them again and toss them a few times to make sure they're all covered.
3. When the machine is ready, pour the sweet potato matchsticks into the basket, spreading them out as evenly as possible. Air-fry the matchsticks for 20 minutes, turning and rearranging them every 5 minutes, until they are lightly browned and crisp.
4. Empty the contents of the basket into a basin, season with salt to taste, and toss to coat.

ROASTED BROCCOLI

Servings: 4

Time to cook: 8 minutes.

Ingredients:

- Broccoli florets, 12 oz.
- 2 tbsp of olive oil.
- 1/2 teaspoons of salt
- 1/4 teaspoons of black pepper, ground

Directions:

1. Preheat the air fryer to 360°F (180°C).
2. Place the broccoli in a medium bowl and sprinkle with oil. Season with salt & pepper to taste.
3. Cook for 8 minutes, shaking the basket twice while cooking, until the outside is golden and the interior is soft in the air fryer basket. Serve hot.

MEXICAN-STYLE FRITTATA

4 servings

Time to cook: 35 minutes.

Ingredients:

- 1/2 cups of Cotija cheese, shredded
- 1/2 cups of black beans, cooked
- 1 cooked potato, sliced
- 3 beaten eggs
- Season with salt & pepper to taste

Directions:

1. Preheat the air fryer to 350 degrees Fahrenheit. In a mixing dish, combine the eggs, beans, half of the Cotija cheese, salt, and pepper. Fill a greased baking dish halfway with the mixture. Serve with sliced potatoes on top. Air fried the baking dish for 10 minutes in the frying basket. Remove the basket and scatter the remaining Cotija cheese over the plate. Cook for 10 minutes more, or until golden and bubbly. Cut into wedges to serve.

DESSERTS AND SWEETS RECIPES

MUFFINS WITH NUTS AND FUDGE

Servings: 10

Time to cook: 10 minutes.

Ingredients:

- 1 package fudges brownie mix
- 1 egg
- Two tablespoons water
- 1/4 cups of chopped walnuts
- 1/3 tablespoons olive oil

Directions:

1. Preheat the air fryer to 300°F and lightly grease 10 muffin cups.
2. In a mixing dish, combine the brownie mix, eggs, oil, and water.
3. Fold in the walnuts and divide the batter among the muffin cups.
4. Bake for 10 minutes with the muffin pans in the air fryer basket.
5. Remove from oven and serve right away.

COCONUT FLAKES, TOASTED

1 serving

Time to cook: 5 minutes.

Ingredients:

- 1 cup unsweetened coconut flakes
- 2 tablespoons melted coconut oil
- 1/4 cups of erythritol granules
- Salt

Directions:

1. Combine the coconut flakes, oil, granular erythritol, and a sprinkle of salt in a large mixing bowl, making sure the flakes are well covered.
2. Place the coconut flakes in your fryer and cook for three minutes at 300 °F, shaking the basket occasionally. Cook until golden and serve.

PASTRIES WITH MARSHMALLOWS

Servings: 8

Time to cook: 5 minutes.

Ingredients:

- 4 oz. melted butter,
- 8 phyllo pastry sheets, thawed
- 1/2 cups of peanut butter, chunky
- 8 tablespoons marshmallow fluff
- 1 teaspoon sea salt

Directions:

1. Preheat the Air Fryer to 360°F and coat a cooking spray-coated Air Fryer basket.
2. Butter 1 filo pastry sheet and top with another filo sheet.
3. Brush the second filo pastry sheet with butter, and then repeat with the remaining sheets.
4. Cut the phyllo layers into 8 strips and spread 1 tablespoon peanut butter and 1 teaspoon marshmallow fluff on each of the filo strips.
5. Fold the sheet's tip over the filling to make a triangle, and then fold in a zigzag pattern.
6. Bake the pastries for 5 minutes in the air fryer basket.
7. Season with salt and pepper to taste and serve hot.

MERENGUE'S

6 servings

Time to cook: 65 minutes.

Ingredients:

- 2 beaten egg whites.
- 1 teaspoon lime zest, grated
- 1 teaspoon lime juice
- Erythritol (four tablespoons)

Directions:

1. Whip the egg whites until they form soft peaks. Then mix in the erythritol and lime juice until the egg whites form stiff peaks. After that, add the lime zest and gently fold it into the egg white mixture. Preheat the air fryer to 275 degrees Fahrenheit. Baking paper should be used to line the air fryer basket. Make the mini merengue's using a spoon and place them in a single layer in the air fryer. Allow 65 minutes to cook the dessert.

APPLE BAKE

6 servings

Time to cook: 20 minutes.

Ingredients:

- 3 tiny Honey Crisp or other baking apples
- 3 tbsp maple syrup
- 3 tbsp. pecans, chopped
- 1 tablespoon firm butter, cut into 6 slices

Directions:

1. Pour 1/2 cups of water into the air fryer drawer.
2. Wash and dry the apples thoroughly.
3. Cut the apples in half. To form a hollow for the pecans, remove the core and some of the flesh.
4. Place apple halves, cut side up, in the air fryer basket.
5. Fill each cavity with 1 1/2 tablespoons of pecans.
6. On each apple, drizzle 1/2 tbsp of maple syrup over the pecans.
7. Drizzle each apple with 1/2 teaspoons of butter.
8. Bake at 360°F for 20 minutes, or until the apples are soft.

CHOCOLATE SOUFFLÉS

Servings: 2

Time to cook: 15 minutes.

Ingredients:

- 2 big eggs, separated whites and yolks,
- 1 teaspoon of vanilla extract
- 2 ounces of chocolate chips (low carb)
- 2 tablespoons of melted coconut oil.

Directions:

1. In a medium mixing bowl, whisk together the egg whites until firm peaks form, approximately 2 minutes. Place aside. In a separate medium mixing bowl, combine egg yolks and vanilla extract. Place aside.
2. Drizzle coconut oil over chocolate chips in a separate medium microwave-safe dish. Microwave on high for 20 seconds, and then swirl and cook in 10-second increments until the chocolate is melted, being careful not to overheat. Allow 1 minute to cool.
3. Slowly pour melted chocolate into the egg yolks, whisking constantly until smooth. Then, gradually add 1/4 cups of the egg white mixture to the chocolate mixture, mixing it gently.

4. Divide the mixture into two 4-inch greased ramekins. Insert the ramekins into the air fryer basket. Set the oven temperature to 400°F and the timer for 15 minutes. Soufflés will bubble up while cooking and collapse somewhat after cooling. When finished, the centre will be established. Allow 10 minutes to cool before serving.

MARMALADE ORANGE

4 servings

Time to cook: 20 minutes.

Ingredients:

- 4 peeled and sliced oranges.
- 3 cups sugar
- 1 1/2 cup of water

Directions:

1. In a pan large enough to fit your air fryer, combine the oranges, sugar, and water; stir.
2. Heat the pan in the fryer for 20 minutes at 340 °F.
3. Thoroughly combine all ingredients, divide among glasses, chill, and serve cold.

BROWNIES WITH CHOCOLATE CHIPS

4 servings

Time to cook: 16 minutes.

Ingredients:

- 1 banana, overripe
- 1 scoop protein powder
- 2 tbsp unsweetened chocolate powder
- 1/2 cup almond butter, melted

Directions:

1. Preheat the air fryer to 325 degrees F.
2. Spray an air fryer baking pan with cooking spray.
3. In a blender, combine all of the ingredients and mix until smooth.
4. Place the batter in the air fryer basket after pouring it into the prepared pan.
5. Bake for 16 minutes the brownie.
6. Plate the dish and serve.

CINNAMON-ROASTED PUMPKIN SEEDS

2 servings

Time to cook: 35 minutes.

Ingredients:

- 1 cup uncooked pumpkin seeds
- 1 tablespoon cinnamon powder
- Two tablespoons sugar
- 1 quart of water
- 1 tablespoon olive oil

Directions:

1. Combine the pumpkin seeds, cinnamon, and water in a frying pan.
2. Bring the mixture to a boil over high heat for 2 to 3 minutes.
3. Drain the water and set the seeds on a clean kitchen towel to dry for 20 to 30 minutes.
4. Combine the sugar, dried seeds, a sprinkle of cinnamon, and one tablespoon of olive oil in a mixing dish.
5. Preheat the air fryer to 340 degrees F.
6. Place the seed mixture in the fryer basket and cook for 15 minutes, stirring the basket occasionally.

STRAWBERRIES ON CUPCAKES

8 servings

Time to cook: 10 minutes.

Ingredients:

- 16 halved strawberries
- 2 tbsp of coconut oil.
- 2 cups chocolate chips, melted

Directions:

1. Toss the strawberries with the oil and melted chocolate chips in a pan that fits your air fryer, then place the pan in the air fryer and cook at 340°F for 10 minutes. Serve it chilled in individual glasses.

RECIPE FOR MUG BROWNIES

1 serving

Time to cook: 10 minutes.

Ingredients:

- 1 scoop chocolate protein powder
- 1 teaspoon cocoa powder
- half tsp. baking powder
- 1/4 cup unsweetened almond milk

Directions:

1. In a cup, combine the baking powder, protein powder, and cocoa powder.
2. Fill a cup halfway with milk and thoroughly mix it.
3. Cook the cup in the air fryer for 10 minutes at 390 °F.
4. Plate the dish and serve.

CAKE WITH LEMON RICOTTA

8 servings

Time to cook: 40 minutes.

Ingredients:

- 1 pound ricotta cheese
- 4 eggs
- 1 teaspoon lemon juice
- 1 tsp. lemon zest
- 1/4 cups of erythritol

Directions:

1. Preheat the air fryer to 325 degrees F.
2. Coat the baking dish in the air fryer with cooking spray.
3. Cream the ricotta cheese in a mixing bowl until smooth.
4. Gradually whisk in the eggs.
5. Add the lemon juice and zest and mix well.
6. Pour the batter into the baking dish that has been prepared and set it in the air fryer.
7. Leave to steam for 40 minutes.
8. Allow it to cool fully before slicing and serving.

Banana Pastry with a Heart

Servings: 2

Time to cook: 15 minutes.

Ingredients:

- Three tablespoons honey
- 2 sheets of puff pastry cut into thin strips
- Garnish with fresh berries.

Directions:

1. Preheat your air fryer to 340 degrees Fahrenheit.
2. Fill the frying basket halfway with banana slices. Cover with pastry slices and drizzle with honey. 10 minutes in the oven for garnish, use fresh berries.

Bread with Monkeys

Servings: 6

Time to cook: 20 minutes.

Ingredients:

- 1 chilled cookie dough can
- Granulated sugar, 1/2 cups
- 1 tbsp. cinnamon powder
- 1/4 cups of melted salted butter
- 1/4 cups of granulated sugar
- Spray cooking oil on

Directions:

1. Preheat the air fryer to 325 degrees F. cooking spray on a 6-inch circular cake pan. Separate the biscuits and cut them into four pieces each.
2. In a large mixing bowl, combine granulated sugar and cinnamon. Toss the biscuits in the cinnamon-sugar mixture until well covered. Place one biscuit in each prepared pan.
3. Combine the butter and brown sugar in a medium mixing basin. Distribute the mixture equally over the biscuit pieces.
4. Cook for 20 minutes, or until golden brown, in the air fryer basket. Allow the bread to cool for 10 minutes before turning it out of the pan and serving.

Lime Muffins with no flour

Servings: 6

Time to cook: 30 minutes.

Ingredients:

- 2 tablespoons lime juice and zest
- 1 cup yoghurt (Greek)
- 1/4 cup granulated sugar
- 8 ounces of cream cheese.
- 1 tablespoon vanilla extract

Directions:

1. Preheat the air fryer to 330°F and mix the yoghurt and cheese with a spatula. In a separate dish, combine the other ingredients. Fold the lime into the cheese mixture gently. Divide the batter into 6 muffin cups that have been lined with paper liners. Cook for 10 minutes in the air fryer.

Midnight Nutella Banana Sandwich

2 servings

Time to cook: 8 minutes.

Ingredients:

- Softened butter
- 4 white bread slices.
- 1/4-cup hazelnut chocolate spread
- One banana

Directions:

1. Preheat the air fryer to 370 degrees Fahrenheit.
2. Spread softened butter on one side of each piece of bread and place it greased side down on the counter. On the opposite side of the bread pieces, spread the chocolate hazelnut spread. Cut the banana in half, and then slice each half into three lengthwise slices. To prepare two sandwiches, layer the banana slices on two pieces of bread and top with the remaining slices of bread. Cut the sandwiches in half to put them all in the air fryer at once. Place the sandwiches in the air fryer to cook.
3. Cook for 5 minutes at 370°F in an air fryer. Flip the sandwiches over and continue to air-fry for 2 to 3 minutes, or until the top bread slices are well browned. While the sandwiches cool somewhat, pour yourself a glass of milk or a midnight nightcap and enjoy!

CHOCOLATE BOMBS

12 servings

Time to cook: 8 minutes.

Ingredients:

- 2 cups macadamia nuts, chopped
- 4 teaspoons of melted coconut oil.
- 1 teaspoon of vanilla extract
- 1/4 tbsp. cocoa powder
- Swerve 3/4 cup

Directions:

- In a mixing bowl, whisk together all of the ingredients. Form medium balls from this mixture, put them in an air fryer, and cook them at 300°F for 8 minutes. Serve chilled.

FRUIT ROTATIONS

6 servings

Time to cook: 25 minutes.

Ingredients:

- 1 sheet puff pastry dough
- 6 tbsp of peach preserves
- 3 kiwis, sliced
- 1 large beaten egg
- 1 teaspoon of icing sugar

Directions:

1. Cut the puff pastry into six rectangles. Roll the pastry into 5-inch squares using a rolling pin. Place one square on your desk so that it resembles a diamond with points at the top and bottom. Spread 1 tsp of preserves on the bottom half, leaving a 1/2-inch border around the perimeter. On top of the preserves, place half of a kiwi. Brush the clean edges with the egg, and then fold the top corner of the triangle over the filling. To seal the pastry, crimp it with a fork. Brush the egg over the top of the pastry. Heat the air fryer to 350°F. Place the pastries in the frying basket that has been oiled. 10 minutes, turning once, until golden and fluffy. Remove from the fryer; allow cooling, and then dusting with icing sugar. Serve

OREOS FRIED

12 servings

Time to cook: 6 minutes for each batch.

Ingredients:

- Spraying oil or non-stick spray
- 1 cup ready-made pancake and waffle mix
- 1 teaspoon of vanilla extract
- 1/2 cup water plus 2 teaspoons
- 12 chocolate sandwich cookies, such as Oreos,
- 1 tbsp. confectioner's sugar

Directions:

1. Coat a baking pan with oil or non-stick spray before placing it in the basket.
2. Preheat the air fryer to 390 degrees Fahrenheit.
3. Combine the pancake mix, vanilla extract, and water in a medium mixing basin.
4. Dip four cookies in the batter and lay them out on the baking sheet.
5. Cook for 6 minutes, or until golden brown.
6. Steps 4 and 5 should be repeated for the remaining cookies.
7. Sprinkle sugar on top of the hot cookies.

TWINKIES FRIED

Servings: 6

Time to cook: 5 minutes.

Ingredients:

- 2 pound egg white (s)
- 2 tablespoons water
- 1 1/2 cups of gingersnap cookie crumbs
- Six Twinkies
- Spray with vegetable oil.

Directions:

- Preheat the air fryer to 400 degrees F.
- Arrange and fill two shallow soup or small pie plates on your counter: one for the egg white(s), whisked with the water until frothy, and one for the gingersnap crumbs.
- Coat both sides of a Twinkie in the egg white(s), including the ends. Allow the extra egg white mixture to blend back into the remainder of the batter before placing the Twinkie in the crumbs. Roll it to cover all surfaces, including the ends, gently pressing to provide a uniform coating. Repeat with the egg white(s), then the crumbs. Spray the prepared Twinkie lightly with vegetable oil spray on both sides. Set aside and repeat the double-dipping and spraying method with the remaining Twinkies.

- Place the Twinkies in the basket flat side up, with as much air space between them as feasible. Cook for 5 minutes, or until browned and crispy.
- Gently transfer the Twinkies to a wire rack using a non-stick spatula. Allow at least 10 minutes to cool before serving.

LEMON BERRIES IN A STEW

4 servings

Time to cook: 20 minutes.

Ingredients:

- 1 pound strawberries cut into halves
- 4 teaspoons of stevia
- 1 teaspoon of lemon juice.
- 1–1/2 cup water

Directions:

1. Combine all of the ingredients in an air fryer-compatible pan, stir, and cook at 340 °F for 20 minutes. Serve the stew cold in individual glasses.

DELECTABLE VANILLA CUSTARD

2 servings

Time to cook: 20 minutes.

Ingredients:

- 5 eggs
- Swerve (two tablespoons)
- 1 teaspoon vanilla extract
- 1/2 cups of almond milk, unsweetened
- Half cup of cream cheese

Directions:

1. In a mixing basin, beat the eggs using a hand mixer.
2. Beat in the cream cheese, sweetener, vanilla extract, and almond milk for 2 minutes more.
3. Lightly coat two ramekins with cooking spray.
4. Pour the batter into the ramekins that have been prepared.
5. Preheat the air fryer to 350 degrees F.
6. Cook the ramekins for 20 minutes in the air fryer.
7. Plate the dish and serve.

Printed in Great Britain
by Amazon

16474238R00043